CORNER OF
DIVISADERO
AND WHATEVER

CORNER OF DIVISADERO AND WHATEVER

Kevyn Clark

To order additional copies of this book, contact:
Xlibris Corporation
1-888-7-XLIBRIS
www.Xlibris.com
Orders@Xlibris.com

CONTENTS

To my family

To my friends

To all of the people I owe money to,
let us pray.

For all of us
still in the dark
waiting.

forward

Kevyn,
I told you I'd write you a letter as soon as I got settled. Well I'm settled and things suck. I don't know why the hell I listened to you about getting together with Mary and moving out here. I liked Dallas just fine. Chicago sucks. You suck. I hope you die. And as far as me writing anything for that stupid book, KISS MY ASS!
Mark Kensington/Roadie 1955-1980

Dear Kevyn.
I just now got the post card from Los Angeles. You seem to be doing fine. Carolyn says thank you for the lovely poetry and wonders when you're going to get serious about your writing. If you haven't heard from Mark or Thomas yet, I had a small heart attack. Nothing big but I had to stop driving for a bit. I'm sure I'll get back out there pretty soon and we'll meet up again at some show or something. It was really a lot of fun touring with you. See you in the future.
Hank Meyers/Truck Driver 1947-1980

Yo Madman Kevyn!
How are you man? When are you going to get a phone? I had a job lined up for you here in Boston but I couldn't get ya man! Allesha and I GOT MARRIED!!!!
That's a total kick in the head huh? You were right Kevyn, I needed this, I needed her. Anyway Madman, we're moving out to Vancouver next week, yeah another big fucking change, but I have a job there and Allesha has the house too. You better get your ass

up there before too long man! It's already been way too long! We need to party! I hope your writing is going well. I liked the last poem I got. It was way weird Madman.
Thomas Wookster/Roadie 1952-1980

"Why don't you bring your axe over and we can jam? I've got some Jack and stuff, we haven't seen each other and I'd like to talk. Maybe we could start writing a few things."
Kyle Clark 1953-1980

Yeah! Welcome to Kevyn's nightmare. I only call it that because some of you wont be able to pick off the scab of filth and vulgarity that covers the real raw meat of this poetry. Some people will get hung up on the coarse nature of what Kevyn has to say, or the form of poetry itself. Look a little further into Kevyn's soul, and your own for that matter. You may not like what you see at first but believe me; there *is* beauty there.

I'm excited to be adding to the forward of Kevyn's book. I'm in great literary company here. I wasn't his first choice, but I am writing part. It actually makes sense. I've seen Kevyn at his best and worst.

Let me tell you a story about Kevyn. There he is working some metal show; you know, teenage boys banging their heads into walls and bimbos in mini skirts, high heels and big hair. All of the stage-hands get these 'working' stick on passes so they can run around without getting hassled too much from the security fucks. Now every once in a while, when the situation arises, stagehands have been known to give one of these passes to one of the bimbo types. Actually give is the wrong word, more like barter. Anyway, the going rate for one of these passes is head. A blowjob. It's sort of an unwritten law.

So, at this show this bimbo type approaches Kevyn with a big smile, eyes his pass, then his crotch and says real breathy like, "I'd do anything, anything at all if you could get me backstage. The lead singer is a friend of mine but he doesn't know that I'm here yet."

"Anything?" asks Kevyn

"ANYTHING" she says.

So Kevyn says, "I love your shoes. Give me your shoes and you can have my pass."

The last thing Kevyn sees of her is her ass as she's running away screaming what a sick dog Kevyn is. This lady wouldn't have any trouble blowing a complete stranger, but she wouldn't give up the pumps. Kevyn is the sick one?

Anyway, that's what I mean. Each of us is boxed in by our own experiences. Our perception of things is completely skewed by the filters in our mind, the box of remembered experience.

Think out of the box.

Remember what it was like to find something new.

Read Kevyn's book.

Don't let poetry fool you.

It's about Kevyn and you and me and all of our lives.

If you find after reading this book that you've stepped in something a little to foul for your liking, just wipe it off on your neighbors lawn and trudge on. I guarantee you'll find something less offensive just ahead.

Ladies and Gentlemen, boys and girls, its LAST CALL for alcohol

See ya later.

Michael Thompson/Bartender 1953-

first poem

Welcome
to the
first poem.
We want you
to be
at home,
relax
a
bit,
take
a load
off,
get
into the mood,
be awake,
aware,
ready to
experience
something,
anything,
ready?
Here
we
go.

And now a word from our sponsors . . .

546-CLAR

for sale

Lay down
the fat
cat
wad
and purchase
this
greasy
mother
fucker
you can't
go wrong
because
inside
is something
for everyone
(except all of the uptight, self-righteous, priggish, self-important,
inflated, money grubbing dipsticks who can't let go of the fat cash
and slide into an easy chair to free the feeling and have a beer or
cola or a smoke or more and slip into the real world and kick it and
open their eyes for a minute because it's important and I might
say something that'll change their lives or at least make them laugh
or maybe think because that's the important part type of person)
and besides,
you can't
get laid
for $25.00
anymore
and my mom

needs
that operation
and
I need a beer
and
we all
need
something.

<u>depression</u>

It's funny
when suddenly
the depression lifts,
flies weird
away
and
without notification,
I
smile
maybe
a laugh even,
but there I am,
feeling
the last
part of the sun
burn away
what remains
of that day,
the cat
nearby zen,
and a breeze
cooling the ground
around
my feet.
I am
here
again
in the best way

and I talk
and walk
and breathe
and play
and the future
is where it should be
and the past is
there too
and I am inhaling the present
into my lungs,
my sick
soul,
hoping again
that this feeling
will stay longer
than the last time.

phone call

Dear sweet god
the sadness and
emptiness
I feel
as if all of creation
has folded,
the final curtain
rung down,
loneliness
squared.
I feel
as if
my heart
has ceased to function
and the last breath
exited my chest.
Oh the want,
the desire,
the pure lust
that I'll never know,
the "what if"
alone
driving me insane.
I guess
I should have
gone ahead
and answered
the phone.
Now
I'll never know.

dreams

I want
to dance free
from all
that bothers me
into your arms
we will lie together
covered in hope
sheets of dreams
and make love as it rains around us.
Hold me
as I shiver
and shake off
my addictions,
bad moods
evaporating
with the morning light,
I kiss your lips
my love.
Let me sleep
a while longer
I'm enjoying
this dream.

what if they killed all the poets

What if they killed all the poets,
the brooding, suffering breed,
or better yet, put them in therapy
and made them account for their deeds.

Tell us the meaning of this one
you whining, arrogant sap,
oh, the beauty, the love, the human condition,
It's all just a big load of crap.

They bore us with rhymes of heartbreak
of reason, and hardier stuff
when we know it's all a barrel of shite
dear poet, we're calling your bluff.

What gives them the right to ponder
on such personal, intimate fare,
while the rest of us humbly grovel
afraid that we're missing our share.

Let's make them take jobs in factories
surrounded by poisons and swill,
let them all slave for a lifetime
then see if they'll still raise the quill.

Let's ridicule, mock and abuse them,
that'd deny them the reason to rhyme
I'm quite sure they'd stop the nonsense
it'd be just a matter of time
oh yes, it'd be just a matter of time.

blackness

Tonight I drink
to the aching,
wallowing in self pity
being swallowed
by some darkness
they've all tried to explain
at some point.
My blackness
belongs to me
and the voices,
the calm
collected
educated voices
with simple line
and
clear
concise
meaning
have no place here
I don't need them
running into things in the dark,
my dark,
besides
I have monsters here
that those calm
collected
educated voices
couldn't begin

to dream about,
my monsters,
meant to haunt and torture me
in my blackness.
I know my way
but for now
I wallow
in the dark
drinking
to the ache.
I will
turn on the light
someday.

crazy

They used to say
that
writing poetry
getting drunk
smoking cigarettes
and dope
staring out windows
fucking off
was artistic
but now
they call it
sure signs
of depression
that are treatable
with medications
that make you
write poetry
get drunk
smoke cigarettes
and dope
stare out windows
and fuck off.
You just have to do it
from the inside of
a plastic
bag.

hard

so hard this life
is so hard
sometimes
it is hard
to even breathe
with
all of the beautiful things
crushing me
stone
after stone
until
it is hard to breathe
even more so
knowing that
it was I
that let those beautiful things
fly
only to have them
come sailing back to me
onto
me it is hard
to be crushed
by beauty
and life
so
hard
it hurts
maybe

I can let go
and
they will
fly
again.

addict

I'm just waiting
for the world to end,
I know the sun will come up
and go down
again
the time in between
spent
in the last throes
of desperation
and craziness
I cannot defend.

I gave up
trying to comprehend,
the rules of life
mean nothing
if I cannot spend
my time
in dense fogs
littered with pieces
of past and present
trying to reassemble them.

So into these depths
I will descend,
chained
to the most brutal love
where I can pretend

that it protects me
from the demons
and devils
and dealers
that begin to lurk
at 4 a.m.

Do not offer
what you will not lend,
I will find the way
to steal
until it all blends
into the small pile
of memories
and things I still have left
that I might
get to keep in the end.

I do not want
the love you send,
the hate I have
echoes loud
though who it offends
does not concern me
because it drowns
all the voices I hear
and the sorrow
with which
I must contend.

Do not try and save me then
my doors are locked
windows shut,
I retreat again
as the curses fade

back to the clouds
that have swallowed me whole
where I will wait
for the world to end.

first impressions

some things
make lasting impressions on us,
we as human beings
are impressionable,
we try to impress upon,
some of us,
myself included,
hope to be impressionistic,
ah but those first impressions
the lasting ones,
those are the ones
I'm talking about,
like a certain sunset
you'll never forget
or the first taste
of strange and delicate delicacies
or your child's first step
or that first car
the first kiss
or walking in
on your first wife
as she's fucking a man
you don't know.
ah,
those first
and lasting impressions.

the wagon

I fumble with a cigarette when I wake up.
Funny,
I wasn't smoking yesterday.
Empty bottles line the desk,
dead soldiers on the battlefield.
What an accurate choice of words,
'Twas a war indeed.

Apparently,
whatever wagon I was on
only had 3 wheels
and tilted quite a bit,
bouncing along
on the way to combat.

the boots

that man
was more than a pair of boots
he was somebody
to someone
somewhere
and yet
he drank away those memories
one glass
at a time
sitting in the bar
on the corner
of Divisadero
and
whatever
where
I used to go
a long
long
time
ago,
watching him
and the other bastards
drink away
whatever they had
and then some
with passion.

one day,
quite like all the rest
for me
and you,
he died
after having his toast
to those lost things
we all lose
but rarely
pay attention to,
and now
his boots
are on my feet.

$27.00
at the second hand store
on Haight
and whatever.

I waited
for his stuff
to come into that store
after he died
so I could feel
his whiskey sours
and bourbons
and martinis
and tequilas
on my feet,
and maybe
so all of those things
that he lost
while he was drinking at that fucking bar

could walk free
and easy
again
one step
at a time.

money

I throw money around like bricks
expecting windows to break
a crash
of diamonds
in my wake
all the while
knowing
that next week
the pebble I have
in my hand
wouldn't leave a welt
of any size or consequence
on my bartenders
head.

the grape

struggling the cork
fighting every millimeter
my intent
is quite
correct
and opened
it breathes
submission
acceptance
and poured
it waits
and I see the hands
withered
and foreign
dirty
with love
picking the contents
of this bottle
I am about to rape
with my
unskilled tongue,
to you,
the growers
and pickers
my worker friends
I will drink.
May you make
Li Po
proud.

morning after

oh dear sweet god
look at that sunrise;
pink and purple
swirls
on a blue gray canvas
hanging there,
if I had religion
I would swear
that all of this
was part of me
and
last night,
the whore
I became,
the drunk
I was,
the things
I did,
would be forgotten
in this dazzling
morning portrait
and jesus
would clean
and scrub away
like surgery,
but
I am still
just a mess,

a whore,
a drunk,
with ashtrays to empty,
a carcass
to remove
from my bed
and
the shakes,
the edginess
and hangover
to handle,
but,
what a beautiful
fucking
sunrise.

the greatest breast ever told

in some bar
somewhere
lost in the cool
smoky
darkness
hiding from a mid-afternoon
of nonsense,
quietly,
someone enters,
passes to the other end
of the long bar
and returns
sitting next to me
and
I notice
the breasts
even before the expensive perfume
and they heave
exploding from
the white tank top
bra-less
the size of
watermelons
and
I can't take my eyes off of
these tits
breathing next to me
until

HE
says
"They did a great job didn't they?"
and the rest of the dark afternoon
was filled
with laughter
and tequila
and recording the stares
and glares
of others
coming and going
watching
him jiggle.

insomnia

A hot
mid-western
midnight wind
whispers boring
impotent lullabies
through my neighborhood.
Searching for sleepy souls,
descending on darkened homes,
it passes me by.

mass

Mozart
Requiem Mass,
how appropriate at 3 am
during another fit of drinking
and drugs.
Not that death
would accomplish anything.
It's just a whim.
Still,
appropriate.

I saw the movie
Amadeus
several times.
I was moved.
Was he really
writing his own mass?
again,
how appropriate.
A whim,
no, perhaps
passion.

My brother
killed himself
without writing a mass.
My sister tried
and failed.

Not enough drinking
I guess.
No requiem mass
for her.

3:20 am
and the music
fills my head.
The cadence,
the measures,
the familiar
notes pounding
on my temples
let me in.
this is for you.

Oh God,
the sweet harmony
dressed in alcohol
and opiates
strumming through
these tired
and aching veins
like weary streets,
closed,
longing for detour.

Over and over
the intricate patterns
play,
my hands sway
conducting,
head bowed
I write my own mass
because I cannot
stop trying to be
appropriate
amen.

driving daniella's lullaby

She says
"You're not an old man,
but you're not a young man any more,
you're somewhere in the middle of something
and we've talked about this before,
and I wont be your lover
and you wont fall in love . . ."
anyway,
pretty soon,
we'll both be home
and this will be over.
Goodnight Danny,
sweet dreams.

So I steal glances
while I'm driving,
trying to make the curves
and I watch her face
as she explains
that we all get what we deserve.
Another hotel,
another night,
and I watch her sleep alone.
I understand she's happy now,
but I'm still shaking to my bones.
Goodnight Danny,
sweet dreams.

I wont ever mention love
because you don't want me to,
all this time
passing by
with so much left to do.
I don't want to spoil the fun
of seeing you this way,
besides,
the mountains we're driving through
could fall
and it wouldn't matter what I say.
Goodnight Danny,
sweet dreams.

By the time
this trip is through
and you're getting on the plane,
we'll both know the reason why
I drive myself insane with this thing.
Still, I can't help watching you
sleeping in that bed,
don't you know
I'd give anything
to be a dream inside your head.
Goodnight Danny
sweet dreams.

(In a million years
I could close my eyes and see your face
and still not know what to do
because the eloquence of promises
denied me a taste of you
so
in parting we will brush our lips,
chaste and full of fear,
you know
it will take a million years
to finally let you go.)
Goodbye Danny,
sweet dreams.

546-CLAR

all the little animals

I know guys
that go fishing,
and hunting,
now don't get me wrong,
I eat meat
but I don't kill it,
I'd rather go to
fish farms
and pet the fishies
"good fish,
go eat some bugs
and stuff"
and I could spend
hours
along side the road
mooing
along with my
bovine brothers
and I know
that animals
like bears
are out there
and I'm quite sure
that if I saw one
up close
in the wild
after cleaning out the mess
in my shorts

I'd be really glad
I saw one
and here's to
all the frogs
and salamanders
that change the course
of freeways
and
I'd like to say
there isn't
a buffalo
that I've met
that I haven't liked
and
I even try to get the spiders
out of the shower
before I turn the water on
and
I moved from
a rat-infested apartment
instead of
calling the exterminator
and I've always tried
to be nice
to my cat
and all of the other
little animals
including
those slimy
roach bastards
that I'd really rather
squash
the shit out of
but don't
because

the cat
will eat them,
natural selection,
and I wont work the circus any more
because that
is slavery
and even though
I've been bitten
I still like dogs
sure little puppy
go chow chow
and even though the birds
wake me up
earlier than I'd like
it's good to hear them too
so
don't go telling me about
all the little animals,
I love 'em,
especially
women.

tonight

"What are you trying to do to me?"
A bottle or two of wine
after a serious lunch
that turned to dinner
and more into evening.
"I want you
to confess your sins,
tell me everything."
She became uneasy.
The light moved across her face
shadows
on narrowed eyes.
Lips tightened,
I could sense
her hesitation.
"I have nothing to hide
no lies
no past
no promises.
I'm nothing more
than what you pour
from that nearly empty bottle."
Watching the last drops fall
into her glass
we shared the moment
where a question
is no longer a question.

muse/bitch

Some muse
the fucker
leaves me stranded
for years
then takes offense
when I force
boozed and opiated
concoctions
up its arse
in retaliation
for leaving me
to find my own voice
behind the fridge
between the cushions
froggy
strained but
still screaming
fucker got fed up
calls itself Patty
working an upscale joint
on some alley
downtown san jose
and instead of
copulating
lifting toasts
she swears
she's moving to Miami
then what?

maybe if I could
pile,
stack,
throw
all the empties
and all of the
continuous erotic possibilities
in front of her
maybe
maybe
she'd stay.
Bitch.

<u>once a king . . .</u>

Young squire
boiling blood
chest ablaze with fury
and faith,
why do you summon
this old warrior?
Another crusade?
Some wrong
against humanity or
sense of dreadful ooze
surfacing
you wish to quell?
Are there
political shenanigans
afoot?
Perhaps
slander?

Dear lad,
look at my wrinkled skin
and shaking hands
my milky eyes
wandering.
I see nothing
but blue skies
my flags
laundry blowing fresh
in the afternoon breeze

castle and moat
filled with delightful maidens,
sailboats
and mermaid breasts.

There will be no battle for me
all of my knights
have turned into day
leaving shield
and sword
piled
carefully under bed
armor folded
into vanities
chain mail
turned to fences
to keep
the rabbits
from the roses.

3 a.m.

Reach over and turn on the light
sit up
get out of bed
find the pants
find the shoes
find the wallet and keys
unlock the door
and lock it behind me
down the stairs
to the laundry room
fumble with the keys
open the door
and lock it behind me
through the laundry room
to the garage door
unlock it
and lock it behind me
open the outside garage door
beep open the car
thinking nothing of the neighbors
back the car out of the garage
into the alley
get out of the car
and close the outside garage door
back into the car
and drive to the end of the alley
take a left onto the street
and a right at the stoplight

straight for 5 blocks
and a right into the parking lot
of the convenience store
get out of the car and beep it locked
into the convenience store
pull out the wallet
pay the man in the turban
while trying to smile
as if I had to apologize
back to the car
beep it open
take a left out of the parking lot
straight for 5 blocks
left at the stop light
right into the alley
get out of the car
open the outside garage door
pull in and park
get out and beep the car locked
screw the neighbors
close the outside garage door
fumble with the keys
open the laundry room door
lock it behind me
go through the laundry room
open the outside door
locking it behind me
climb the stairs
fumble with the keys
open the apartment door
lock it behind me
walk to the bedroom
put the wallet and keys on the dresser
take off the shoes
and pants

climb into bed
and think
all of this
for a God damned
pack of cigarettes.

sleepless

Another sleepless night,
where does it go?
Why does it abandon me?
And I remember
the way the crickets sound
outside of the window
at 4 a.m.
and I remember
the first shades of purple
just a bit later
things
not too difficult to forget
after days
turning to night
after night
after night.
Restless
legs
is what they call it.
when I was a child
I danced my way
to sleep.
Growing older
I now
waltz,
tango,
bugaloo
and twist

the sleepless night away.
They
gave me various pills,
copious amounts
of pills
that work once
but end up allowing me
to dance stoned
lie groggy
and wasted
and tripping
the light fantastic.
I can sit on the balcony
listening for the neighbors' snore
the lucky
bastard

I hope
just once
that all of those sleeping
houses
can see what a great dancer I've become
just once
before I die
from exhaustion
after having taken all of the pills
that don't work.
Fred Astaire
would be proud.

break time

Excuse me
but it's break time
and I think
you should
put down this book,
someplace nice,
and go to the bathroom
and maybe get a drink
have a smoke
if you're so inclined,
stretch your legs
unless you read standing up
then
sit down
and take a load off
whatever you do,
don't worry,
I wont be offended
I'm just a book
you know.

46-CLAR

THESE

DON'T

NEED

WORDS

omit

I remember
being taught
in school
to omit
needless
words.

Dear teacher,
I did it,
now what?

the hearing

In my dream
I am sitting at a small table
without counsel,
nervous and sweating
trying not to bite my nails.
Before me
seated in grandstands of white marble
with bikini clad attendants
are all of the great poets
dressed in tennis outfits
looking rather bored
"Have you suffered heartache?"
one screams, trying to be heard
over the drink orders.
I can't see who it is
and I'm about to answer
yes
when another faceless great
stands and asks
"Have you gone hungry
walking the streets homeless
while freezing to death is what the question
should have been."
There is grumbling from the front row
filled with American and English poets
apparently
placed there to interpret
languages I don't understand.

I still answer yes
quite sure of myself.
"Have you been drunk enough
to pick fights in bars
and then be beaten mercilessly
by those who do not understand you?"
and Hemmingway walks over
with Bukowski, spilling gin on my arm
all three of us scream
yes
and they wink at me
suddenly a door opens
and Bach and Mozart stumble in
"Oops, wrong room" they say drunkenly.
"Composers?"

Everyone laughs as a bikini clad attendant
shows them the way out.
"We want to know about the womanizing!"
The room is filled with the tormented screams
of Emily, Plath,
and all of the French whores
that filled the minds
of great men during the revolution
and the whores who wrote prose between lovers
and the whores who never wrote anything,
the muses
and I bow my head
and someone stands and yells
"Do you have an editor?"
and my mouth falls open
"Do you have a publisher?"
and my mouth goes dry,
there is a low mumbling

rumbling filling the room,
that great chamber
and Whitman yells
"NEXT!"
and I am led from the room
by a bikini clad attendant
who tells me
to keep my day job
as she
slams the door
on my ass
on the way out.

long ago

I remember
hanging out
with Dr. H. Thompson
for a while
during a speaking engagement
once
long ago.
He was late
the crowd was
rowdy.
He came rushing in
with some blonde,
came over to me
(just a stagehand)
took me by the arm
and led me away
whispering manically
"What the fuck should I say?
we're in political turmoil
and all they ever want
to hear
about is drugs."
We both looked back
at the blonde.
"Stripper"
he said.
"Thompson"
I said,

"Whatever you talk about
these clowns
will listen,
have fun."
He looked at me,
then at the blonde,
then the promoter came over.
"God Damn it Thompson!"
The doctor smiled at him
"Ready" he said,
then turned to me,
"Take care of the stripper
and I'll buy you a beer"
before he was whisked
on stage.
He talked about
politics
and they
loved him.
The next night
he was early.
The crowd was late.
"I thought it was 7 p.m."
he said.
"Hey, what's your name?"
I told him
and he introduced me to the blonde
who pulled a quart of scotch
out of her
purse.
Thompson grabbed it,
drank quite a bit
and handed it to me.
I drank quite a bit also.
The promoter came in.

"Thompson,
good,
you're here
I . . ."
The doctor said
"Shut up,
we're busy"
and the blonde
shut the door
of the office
in his face.
Then we talked.
Really talked.
He asked me about
how 'the kids'
these days felt about
the way the world was
heading straight
for the shitter.
I told him
they didn't care,
and that was why
it was all headed for the shitter.
All the while,
the blonde
kept passing the bottle.
After 45 minutes
the promoter almost kicked in the door.
The doctor opened it,
said something to him,
turned and smiled,
said "Showtime" and left.
The blonde walked over and shut the door.
After he spoke
and screamed

and ranted
and raved
at the clueless university students
he ran off stage,
grabbed the blonde and me.
"Where the fuck
is the garage,
quick,
they want to kill me."
I led them
through the various
secret theater doors
and walkways
to the garage.
When we reached
his rental
the doctor
lit a joint,
then another,
then a third
and passed them to me
and the blonde,
who was still smiling at me.
"You should write,"
he said to me.
"you're a smart kid,
you know what you're doing.
We have to go, I still owe you a beer."
And they drove off.
The next day
my boss
wanted to know
why there was
an empty bottle of scotch
and a pair of women's panties
on his desk.

Hey Thompson,
thanks.
I'm writing now,
like a clueless bastard
and
you can forget about the beer.

species

I did some research
on life expectancy
and didn't find much,
I wanted to read
about what animal
lived the shortest time.
I read that
house spiders only live
4 to 5 days.
I wonder if
that's because they get
stepped on.
I wondered if there
was another small
little thing that lived
oh
for maybe a night.
Not that it would really matter
to the poor suckers.

I didn't search very long.
I was tired.
I just wanted to know
if such a thing existed
so I could gloat,
look at me
ya little idiots
I'm alive and you

didn't even get to see
the sun come up.
I'm sure some would say
they deserve more.
I don't care,
look, another one just died
whatever they're called
if they even exist.

jail

I had to admit
the old,
Italian
with the pock marked face
named
Lucky
was a mean fucker
and
we went
around
a bit
for my pillow
and blanket,
and after
ten rounds
that often involved
he and I
banding together
fending off intruders
while
beating each other
bloody,
we sat at a table alone
with him telling me
I could be dead
quick
and me
telling him

to
fuck off quick,
step off
fish
and
after all the nonsense
everyone
in that cell block
was told
to leave me alone
or pay dearly
and I got to keep
my blanket
and pillow.

The only other
time
I fought
anyone
was when I
beat down
2 brothers
for trying to steal
smokes
from Lucky's cell
while he was away.
They paid
dearly
and from then on
I had
espressos
every morning
from the guards
and a pack
a week from

one of Lucky's boys,
as a matter of fact
the only thing
I didn't have
after that
was
the right
to walk away,
go to a bar,
slick some
chick
then go home.
Though
we used to bet
and raise
beers and women
along with the smokes
when we played
poker
it wasn't the same
and Lucky would say
you're doing easy time,
relax
and
he'd give me some hooch
he'd made
under his bed
that we drank
right in front of those damned guards.

Lucky
was right,
I did easy time
and
even after
I got out
of that shit hole
I was doing
easy time
because
every night
I walked away,
went to a bar,
slicked
some chick
and
went home
and I
still drink
in front of
whoever
I want and
sometimes,
I still think about
the wind that will carry me
away someday
into the daylight
where chains
turn to feathers
and barbed fences
balloons.

the day billy wrecked the train

Sunday was the day
we gathered around the rails,
hands fishing in grubby pockets
for coins to flatten,
the stories we'd heard
about destruction of government property
failed to keep us from this task.
Sometimes seconds
before the train would rumble by
blowing dirt and shit everywhere,
the braver of us souls stood
mere inches away from the tons
of steel and wood
shooting past us,
and once it had gone
we'd run to find
whatever was left
of allowances we dared to squander.
And then, there was Billy.

Everyone was scared of Billy.
He was huge for his age,
eleven and already five foot two
one hundred and thirty pounds,
but his dad was bigger
and on most Saturday nights
the neighborhood
would ready itself

for the battles from down the street,
the yelling
the bottles breaking
and then
the sirens,
the only thing
that brought Billy relief
from the monsters
that lived in that house
making him
who he was.

On Sundays
the trains were more frequent.
We had
more time alone
since the winos went to church that day.
Observe the balancing act
pennies, dimes, quarters for the upper class
on the rails,
all the while,
shooting the shit and throwing rocks
at empty bottles
watching Billy
further up the line
dealing with his own type of pain.

One Holy day
we lit a fire with stolen matches.
That was a blast until
some asshole,
probably Brian,
threw the burning sleeping bag
under the wheels of the 3:00
and the sparks set the wild grass smoldering

so we had to run
haul ass out of there
before the cops came.
All the while
Billy ignored us.

One sunday Mary and her friend
danced in their underwear among the weeds
that had re-emerged after the fire.
They wanted to squash their allowance
on the tracks we owned by rights.
This was our turf
and if you wanted in
you had better strut your stuff.
Mary pulled up her bra
just as Billy wandered over
from his personal spot by the switch box
further up and said
"I'm telling your brother"
before he returned to his project.
Whatever that was.

On Tuesday we had a day off
a blessed miracle had closed the school.
He must have prayed
and gotten his answer in spades.
And so it was
the rest of us would never have the chance
to talk about how the police
had to show up at Billy's house
at midnight because of the fight
we all heard but he had to deal with.
And he did
in some odd way,
seeking his revenge

on the rails
digging and breaking and bending
with his hands
and a crowbar he stole
from his bastard father.

The day Billy wrecked the train
we all started for the tracks
as usual,
with our pockets of pennies
jingling,
ready for the sacrifice of coin.
We could already hear
the noon whistle
and ran up the incline
as the engine chugged powerful
past us,
unaware
that Billy
had removed a few vital yards
of the line,
the rail up by his secret place
that had reeked of anger before
was as empty   ,
as a ghost.

The train took a breath
and the engine skipped,
a bounce,
over the void
brakes screaming,
but the empty boxcars danced
and turned
three suddenly side by side
then the tanker

flipping like a drunk as the rest of the train
stopped
sending the caboose
almost up on end
then crashing down
into splinters
all around us.
The noise
turned us to stone,
the sight
was a dream,
and then there was Billy,
walking out of the mess,
swinging the crowbar
screaming
"You should have listened."
All we heard then
was the siren.

<u>castrated</u>

I am castrated by the ideas
sometimes
the words
come so fast
that I miss them
and they end up driving away in stolen cars
and on buses
(the lucky ones get airfare.)
I remember the days
when I ignored all this
shit
and went about my day
and when people asked what I was thinking
I'd lie
and say "nothing"
and hope,
try to forget all of those words
that came to me
so fast
but now
I pay attention.
These words
aren't getting away.
I remember
with malice
and forethought.
I scream
with this voice

long distance to god
next door
to satan
and start to drink again
hoping that
I can forgive myself
if I forget words
while I'm in the shower
and forgive myself
for not typing fast enough
and forgive myself
for having to
work
and I take notes
and I scream
and I rail
at the
force
the sheer energy that drives me

and I have
on occasion
been driven to my knees by that very thing
forced to kneel
in the vomit
in the pages
with all of these words
castrating me
leaving me weak
and bleeding
begging for relief.
Please not so fast,
forgive me for abandoning you
but please
I beg you

give me time
to write this down
without forgetting a line.
these lines
are all I have left
sometimes.

protest

Don't think that it all doesn't mean much.
Be wary of that point of view.
The message you're getting is garbled.
There's something that's not getting through.

Just look at what's happening around you,
all the sickness and death and decay.
It's foolish for you to believe that
it'll all simply just go away.

You must know that it's wrong to hurt family
or to pillage for profit or gain,
so the way that you're thinking is wrong friend.
Some would say that it's fucking insane.

You keep throwing your shit in the clock works
It's no wonder it's all gone askew.
You must give up your tools of destruction,
or I'll physically take them from you

Don't think for a second I'm fooling.
My patience is dangerously thin.
I'd gladly kill you to stop all this nonsense,
and your God would forgive me this sin.

Because life as we know it is sacred,
but there's so little time left you know,
and though I love you like you're my own brother,
I'm pulling the plug on your show.

we're off to war

Our nation is in danger
we're led to believe
by uncaring leaders
who lie and deceive
so its war friends and family
we're off to war.

Kiss your sweethearts goodbye
then promise return
praise to glory and honor
here's to medals we'll earn
its a war my sweet fellows
we're going to war

They'll train us for killing
for protection of right
may our enemies tremble
in the face of our might
we'll give them war God Damn it
we'll give them war.

We'll travel the distance
to some foreign land
to be cursed in a language
we don't understand
but that is war, that's why we're here
that is war

In this, the first battle
our enemies near
we've all become children
swallowed by fear
this is war mom and dad
this is war

The fighting's begun
total chaos ensues
are we right if we win
are they wrong if they lose?
But the war's just begun friends
war's just begun

Here things have happened
that time will not mend
bullets and bombshells
have killed all my friends
I hate this war, Jesus Christ
I hate this war

On the bloodiest battlefield
I sit alone
I've been killing my brothers
please send me home
I wont fight this war any more
I wont fight this war.

A man returns home
one fine sunny day
"I thought it was right"
was all he could say
because it was war he would cry
because it was war.

There's no victory in war
to this very day
in the worlds cemeteries
you'll find the price we all pay
for our wars you calloused bastards
for our wars

So put the stars in the windows
flags half mast on the pole
shiny granite above
with little soldiers below
because we went to war, oh dear God,
we went to war.

paranoia

We're all here
just vegetating,
they're coming to get us
and we're just waiting,
we're caught in traps
that they've been baiting,
like children un-prepared,
let's all be real scared.

We seek the truth
but they're all lying,
we turn our backs
but they keep spying,
we cannot hide
from all this prying
but it's time we finally cared,
let's all be real scared

They socialize us
till we're not feeling,
there's no way to tell
just what they're scheming
I'm not asleep
so I'm not dreaming,
it's war that's un-declared,
let's all be real scared.

They make us live
so we all have vices,
and once we do
they raise the prices,
if we try and change
it creates some crisis,
but it's time we finally dared,
let's all be real scared

the law

I'm sure there is a law
that clearly states
"Poetry
pertaining to
an individual's take
on any given subject
especially
love
heartbreak
and rejection
must be written
under the influence
of alcohol
and
that
said poet
must regularly
undertake the practice
of drinking
until intoxicated
prior to
and or
during
the writing process."
and if there isn't
a law
like that
there should be.

546-CLAR

early bird

What kind of bird
is up at 3
in the morning?
He sits in his tree
quite close
calling out
"This tree is
mine"
as if I cared.
that bird
is the reason
I'm awake.
earlier
I heard him yell
"Over here
stupid."
I'm sure
he was talking
to a friend
but
I'm still sitting here
waiting.

I'm awake you bastards

The birds wake me up.
The bastard birds
always wake me up
I don't even set my alarm
anymore
they are so damned loud.
Awake
now what.

coffee

Rituals
don't forget the teeth
S-t-r-e-t-c-h-i-n-g nude
in front of large open windows
facing the street
I watch the 8 o' clock
"I'm late" dance
performed by frenzied neighbors
who are quite sure
they set their birds correctly
the night before.

coffee

I waddle
therefore I am
in the bedroom getting dressed

in old Levis
and grungy t-shirt,
my holy vestment
for the day sermon.
I wear black at night.
flip on the magic box and
colored chaos dances
(I really have to clean this damn monitor)
maybe later.

Coffee
cigarettes, advertisements
and bastard birds for breakfast.
Another swell day in paradise
begins.

monday

Stranger than friction
still
larger than life rafts
sagging and heaving
the entire way
plodding
footfalls through canyons
knee deep in mud
squishy
and
thick
it's the charge of the light brigade
of idiots
foaming mouths agape
compasses pocketed
bananas peeled
and at the ready
tuned to channel
seven
and engines revving
shaved, showered
and stitched
quite succulent
knickers fixed
laces knotted
rolling up the hill
caffeined
sugarless

and deep fried
donut holders frantic
toothless
wanderers
with bound breasts
and shriveled dicks
facing the firing squad.
Out the door
and off to work
on monday.

the love of it all

ah this great society
so willing
to send us all
into battles
of faith
while they collect rent

measure the victories
against the dead
count them every one
this battle
that cause
which do you recall

torn and ripped to shreds
yet still standing
feats of iron will
and blood
I survived
and you did too

remember the dances
of heart and soul
and the rest
the fever
of joy
gave us all of this

yet we stand bare
against this onslaught
this great socialization
shivering cold
gored hard
for the love of it all

what if

I wonder if
in this day and age
Mozart
would have had his ass kicked
by the bullies
on the playground
just because he was weird.
He'd go home
lunch money robbed
eye blackened
books muddied
and old Leopold
would throw fits
calling the principal
attempting to teach
Amadeus
a few punches
and as a last resort
walk him
to school,
an added embarrassment
that would follow him
through
glee club
and haunt him
during
phys ed,
the poor kid.

things to do

Gee, I'm sorry
I'm just not available
today you see,
I've got to
surf with Che' Guevara
play tidily winks with Poe
drag race haul ass down Main Street with Tolstoy
Queen Victoria waving the checkered flag
play ping-pong with Kundun
His Holiness
match point big guy,
by the way,
have you seen Siddartha's new
matching luggage?
Have tea with Satan
(again)
go bowling with Bukowski
shit
seven-ten split
dance with Emily Dickinson
after balling Sylvia Plath
have beers with Rabin
on the Sabbath
play poker with Elvis and Lennon
and Lenin
the pot's light,
head under the bleachers
and peek

with Mozart and Degas
(check the ass on that one)
tattoo Hitler
with a railroad spike
(this might hurt a bit asshole)
tackle football
with Warhol
Marx, Karl keeping score
Marx, Groucho
coach of course
go swimming with Monet
lap after lap
after dining with Gandhi
in Paris
all 9 courses
volleyball with Gompers
squash with old Abe
arm wrestle Satchmo
play marbles with Ginsberg
Take Garbo to a Dead concert
just for a hug
Shine the shoes of Cesar Chavez
(what else could a workingman want?)
have sex with Anne Frank
in an open field
and be there to tell brother King
to duck.
So maybe
some other time.

amadeus

T'is a whisper of voices
moving my soul,
Confutatis
coming
Lacrimosa,
Amadeus,
Mozart,
classical
crap
to most of you.
Stick it in my ear
and wallow
thick.
A few glasses
and a smoke or two
with the headphones
and your world
no longer applies.
You
no longer
exist.
Powdered wigs,
pigs
in the street
and chasing
Amadeus
is all there is.

welcome to the machines

(Sit, I said SIT! Good boy)
What's the matter?
We can't provide the answer to that.
Call the 800 number.
Jump through the hoops.
(Roll over. I said ROLL OVER. Good boy.)
That isn't our department.
Call the 800 number.
We don't handle complaints here.
It takes 90 days.
We never got the completed form.
(BEG!)
You have to go to window 9 for that.
(Good boy.)
Call the 800 number.
Closed after 4 p.m. and on weekends.
Sue whom?
Local social services might help.
Call the 800 number.
(Fetch the stick.)
The computer's down.
You should have talked to,
We can give you an appointment in 90 days.
To file a grievance,
Call the 800 number.
(Stay. I said STAY!)
For more useless time-consuming information press 9.
That number is no longer in service.

I'm sorry, she's on vacation.
I can't seem to find your file.
(Heel. I said HEEL! Bad boy.)
Call the 800 number.
For more information contact.
I'd like to help, have you tried,
Press 1 to return to the main menu.
How do you spell that last name?
We're not allowed to give out that information.
(Shake. I said SHAKE!)
Call the 800 number.
For all inquiries please call,
Can you hold please?
You have the wrong department.
We've already sent the forms.
You forgot to sign on page 38.
Please leave a message after the tone.
Call the 800 number.
(Play dead)
GOOD BOY

working class

I have
a job.
More than
a lot of
you
can say.
They pay
me good
and
I have
benefits.
I don't
have to
worry
about my
kid
getting sick
and I
don't even
have a
kid but
if I
did
I wouldn't
worry.
I have
a car
a Harley

credit cards
and a
cat.
So even
if they
got sick
I wouldn't
worry.
Some people
I know
have houses
they bought
years ago.
In San Jose
that's good
for a smile
these days.
They don't
worry
See?
If you
had a
job
you could
be like
us
and not
worry
so much
and I don't
want to
hear about
your problems
just because
you don't

have legs
or arms
or eyes
or teeth
doesn't mean
you can't
work and
take care
of
your problems.
This is
America
get a
job and
stop worrying
so much.

injured reserve

I am sitting on the bench
injured reserve
thinking back
about my broken body
the memories of pain
come rushing to meet me
like an old friend.

The first one was
the appendix
when I was 13
walking home at 6 a.m.
bent, hardly breathing
maybe 4 miles in all,
they yanked it just in time.

Then there was the hernia
boot camp,
the caring captain,
take the pain
or start over
and I did it bulge and all
meaner than the rest put together.

Then the wrist went,
broken 4 times
in less than 1 year,
they never let it heal

and another
caring captain,
get over it soldier, you'll live.

The knee was next,
dacron ligament
3 hours on the table,
a retired major
let me have
all of the morphine
I wanted, bless him.

The back was sneaky
it came and went
again and again and,
they said something
was crushed,
and if it hurt,
don't do it if you can.

The ankle is my favorite,
3 pins,
2 plates
and a bone graft,
they read my records
and gave me
all the morphine I wanted.

The ribs were something,
can't breathe,
can't move,
2 busted
and 4 internal organs
bruised and battered,
bring on the heroin baby.

They said my toe
was nothing
but gout
until they removed
a bone chip
the size of dallas
after a year of complaining.

The minor ones,
the broken toes,
broken fingers,
and shot twice,
knifed once,
it all adds up,
stitches and glue, screws and wire.

Injured reserve,
they know
I'll still do it,
I know I still can,
better than them all,
it just hurts a bit
and the morphine is gone.

politics

something so pure
white light
with eyes closed
can you hear me?
this shakes your bones
rattles your glasses
wake up
pass it on
fucker
this isn't literature,
it is
blood and bone
sanctified
evil eye
and dining
this is nigger
and
pure white fucking trash
gray meat
and spic and wop and
dago and nip
and rag head
pecking your soulless heart
this is something
you don't want to miss
colorless yet
so well defined
and chosen

You point that gun
at me
and it isn't even you
trying to pull the trigger
you rob me
and you don't even know
who you're stealing from
you can't question
driven by society
that invisible hand
and voice
you have no idea
who is speaking to you
in the tone
and verse
that would make you
kill your own brother
ask why you're blinded

ask why
we're in trouble
my friend
the question is
can we
as skin
touch lips
and promise ammunition
to defeat
this disease
this infestation of inhumanity
climbing our backs
rifling pockets
and stealing our children
convincing

conniving
cowards
daring to turn us
the bone
the soul
against
us

don't close your eyes
don't close your eyes
politics
is killing us my love

boxes

look at my box
my box is
much prettier
than yours
it is
much
bigger
than yours
it is much more
expensive
than yours
I have another box
that is faster
than yours
grander
than yours
and I use it
to take me
to my box
in the country
where I will sit
thinking
about
how I can
get more
boxes
and once I do
I'll rent them
to you.

new ride

Impulses are best
not ignored,
besides
it was purple
and chrome.
Lots of chrome.
That's the way
I like them.

I was sure
that whatever credit
I could muster
wouldn't be enough
but they surprised me
and 3 hours later
I listened
as the guy,
Bob
tried to do his job
by telling me
how to treat
my new Harley
even though I've
already had 14
of the damn things
so we both played
along.

"I prefer the big bikes"
is what he said
while I was waiting
for the right temperature
and the metal to breathe
and the oil to flow.
"I understand"
I said
"But you can't
take a big bike
through 2 parked cars
laying over 30 degrees
at 70 mph either
can you?"

Screaming out of
the parking lot
I almost totally
forgot
my new purple
and chrome
whore
was a virgin.
It was a lovely day for a ride.

words lost during a ride

On some sunny
cold day
on the bike
knowing I should have stayed home
writing
instead of screaming around
pissing off this valleys'
residents,
the 75-mile per hour wind
blowing all of the words
that should have ended up here
onto windshields
of cars
I flew past
occasionally,
one or two of the ideas,
phrases,
thoughts
probably made their way
into an open window
into the head
of some unsuspecting
driver
who was forced to pull over
and wonder
where the hell
did that come from.

blowing kisses at the black watch

on any given day
we're there
all of us
one at a time
we make it,
serious
silly
drunk
sober
horny
and
haughty
to the black watch bar,
on motorcycle weekends
the hordes of monsters
parked howling
side by side,
daring
pedestrians to peer
while we,
us
soldiers
pound beers
or vodkas
or tequilas
or all of it
back
part of the circus

we are inside,
acrobats
balancing bravado
and seduction
between trips
to piss
and pass
the blondes
the redheads
the brunettes
the breasts
and the sluts
waiting for the harley horseman
to offer up a saddle
or a cock
or a drink
as we silently sing
the chorus
a good woman is hard to find
a bad one hard to lose
between the breaths
we take
on those days,
the revelry broken
by silent cheers
as one of us
two of us
or all of us
start up
any combination,
rattling the bottles on the bar
and the nerves
of the neighbors
we toast goodbye
safe ride

as we slip away
like rockets
one by one
until only the bartender
and a few stragglers,
pedestrians,
civilians unwanted
are left inside
with the gore of battle
all around them.

last ride

In majestic slow motion
taillights flash red
brakes are stomped,
grabbed.
In the time it takes the world to rotate on its axis three times,
tires lock and slip
on dark
wet
pavement.
Five hundred pounds of machine
and one hundred and seventy pounds of blood and flesh
twist and tumble,
bike and body dance together.
Seasons pass
as the motorcycle slams to the pavement
onto
the rider,
stars spin
shooting into space
orion,
man and machine wrestle,
grapple,
flipping and flailing
together they slide into home plate
thirty feet further down the road
in a screech of steel
and pain
and as the last of the dust

dirt
and echoes pass into the night,
bike lying
broken diamonds
bleeding gasoline,
the rider opens his eyes one last time
to acknowledge
the rising crescendo of applause
that fills his head.
It is a standing ovation.
Thank you
and
goodnight.

last rites for muscle head

Ain't it strange that you are gone
and I'm standing on your bones?
You're dead and buried underfoot:
part of dirt and stones.
They all figured I'd die first
burnt out and far from home,
so ain't it strange that you are dead
and I'm standing on your bones.
(Ashes to ashes, dust to dust,
get his ass in the ground and away from us.)

goodbye

Oh stop wondering.
This isn't about you.
Don't be so selfish.
What this is about
is the end of wonder.
Try to imagine that
everything you've wanted
everything you could
possibly desire, crave,
want, in your life
is there, presented,
available. What's left?
It's not a bad thing.
What this is
is looking at pictures
that you're in
every one capturing
moments that fill you
with joy, love, peace
and wonder
that can't be captured again
because it's spent,
an empty capsule
and instead of sadness
and regret for times passed
you're filled with
images that replay
all of the moments

in your life
and the end of the movie
is here.
Academy aside,
it was a great film
but its time to go.
That's what this is.
It's that point in life
where you look down
and all you see is the ground
instead of a path
where the sky
looks all too familiar
at sunset
and you skip the sunrise
because your presence
would steal something
from everyone else,
I can share.
I'm just tired
and it doesn't matter
how much sleep I have.
I'll still be tired.
So
my friend,
don't take this personally,
but I have to be going.
Please don't interfere,
a morning filled with
police
and intravenous life
and tubes
seems so boring
in comparison with
what I don't know.

14 days of in depth
psychiatric discussion
followed by months of serious
therapy
is so fucking common place,
irksome.
There is nothing I haven't done
that I want to do
anymore, besides,
I've learned to live without
what I want
and can't have.
Don't be sad.
I saw the sun today.
I felt the heat from that
and a woman I'll never know.
Life was good.
Next.

death has lunch at the cafe

I saw an old man
today
sitting alone
in a non-descript
café nearby
watching
an ancient waitress pour coffee.
He noticed me staring
and frowned,
speaking just above a whisper
he said
"The only reason
you see me
is because
we've nearly met."
I was short of breath,
suddenly confused.
The old man
held up a hand,
"This is filled with
a billion oceans of tears,
countless heartaches,
eternal sadness and regret."
He held the other hand
to his face
closed his eyes saying
"This is filled with love,
compassion, freedom from

pain and suffering."
Opening his eyes,
now filled with tears
hands placed palms down
on the table
he glanced at his feet.
"I have walked
every funeral procession,
danced on every funeral pyre
since time began.
I've cried at every one."
I tried not looking
into his weeping eyes,
those black watery holes
under furrowed brows
but his gaze paralyzed me.
"I thought today
I was finished,"
he said
"I thought today
I was done.
Do you know
how tired of this I am?"
The waitress
walked slowly to his table.
"My shift is over."
The old man stood
and taking the waitress by the hand
walked out the door
into the street.
The next day
the café was closed
for the funeral.

no place like home

Remembering the first words
I learned to read,
a plaque on the wall
by the door of the first house we moved from,
and every place after.
"I like to see a man
proud of the place in which he lives.
I like to see a man live
so that his place will be proud of him."
Profound words that followed us
from home to home.
Even boxed,
packaged
and ready to go
Abraham Lincolns' verse
fit like a glove.
So proud this moving van.

Daydreaming,
face pressed against the car window
watching a boy
then teen
then man
run gazelle like along side our car.
Waving, smiling,
vanishing and re-appearing ghostlike
through buildings,
obstacles we drove by.

I wonder now,
somewhat inert,
if that lad was my memories
of places departed,
trying to catch up,
saying
don't forget the home you left.

And we drive
and we drive,
settling long enough
to find ourselves on a map,
drawing lines from there to here,
and there and over there,
a cobwebbed chart,
veined with the routes
and roads
we have yet to drive
but will.

Before long, forgetting things became simple.
A year would pass
in a month or two
and the whole of our glorious lives
would be packed away again.
Stray marbles
and a piece of string or two
reminders to new tenants that we had passed through,
the back yard trees
nooks and crannies
forgotten in lieu of new adventure
and the names
of those faceless classmates
quickly exchanged
for road signs

license plates and
truck stop menus.

Trying to remember faces
tying them to places
a lost art for me.
I remember a few addresses
maybe a phone number
but the first kiss,
the first date,
the first cigarette,
all those great moments
are gone,
moved from place to place
and finally
nothing,
somewhere out there,
on the roads we traveled
they are missing.

I don't have many close friends
to this day.
No community so to speak.
I never learned how and it seems
all my attempts
to introduce myself to those things
is just sheer vanity.
All of those things were attachments
and even if I wanted them back
it's too late,
they've been traded
for the experience of going,
moving, on the road.

Our parents complain now,
so much time since a visit,
so far away.
Perhaps they shouldn't have given us
so many choices,
of places distant,
so many tastes of this world
that we would choose
something
and someplace
foreign to them.
Did they forget?
Did they forget
the smell of brown boxes
and packing blankets,
the rush of air through
car windows,
the beauty
of cheap hotel neon
at midnight
and being the new person
all the time?

the roadie life

We are cemeteries,
filled with thin white lines
I know that
nothing grows
underneath
where the sun won't shine.
I have
pale white skin,
I see
rainbow colors,
I've felt
long distant hate,
and had
love that smothers.
At the mirror
what I see,
are all the ghosts
staring back at me

I have
empty pockets,
and a crashing heartbeat,
I go through the front door
but walk the back street.
I have
shattered lives,
and stolen souls,
it was the

midnight kisses,
the changing roles.
I've seen preachers lying
as beggars steal,
I'm just a crazy bastard
spinning wheels

One day
I thought I had
a piece of you,
and the persistent demons
it all seemed so true
Now,
I wake up lonely
but I'm getting higher,

it's like
time for sale
but without a buyer
of all the cheap sex
the greatness
the overkill,
livings were made
we just
picked up the spill.
Empty madman make us great,
pick and axe,
I participate
all the while
being shell shocked
and hungry

I got in line,
to suck the whiskey
and fuck the wine.
We can't get laid,
remember that?
so it was fall in love
just drop a hat.

We have
distant memories
of drunken glory,
of smoked out rooms
and half told stories
of bars and scars
and blurry pictures,
it's like
a where house
of unholy scriptures.
Twenty five years my friend
could I forget you?
That foggy daze
bet that I had to.
So we
push the shit
dream saxophone,
tune guitars
while we lose at home.

All those countless faces
and backstage passes,
broken hearts
and lipsticked glasses.
Happy trails my lovers
we all got fed!
I wish I could share
but they're all dead.

And I remember everything.
I close my eyes and you come into view.
I put out my hand
and I could be touching you.
And I remember everything.

rock star, roadie, cherry

Summertime's coming
we'd better start running
we've got 50 cities to play before fall,
and as long as the kids go
we'll give 'em a good show
hell, without all this nonsense I got nothing at all.

So it's hippied out twirlies
and glassy eyed girlies
with brains full of bong water waiting in line.
I guess that could be the hotel
but hell, how can I tell,
I'm on booze, coke and cigarettes most of the time.

(Chorus)
C'mon cherry we'll ride off to glory
though we might not remember too much of the story.
We'll hide from the shadows of the valleys we ride through,
and we'll carry that monkey
just as far as we have to.
Yeah!

Shimmering streetlights
I'm counting the midnights
that push me along to the first light of day.
If I wasn't so phony
I wouldn't be lonely,
if I wasn't so high I might have something to say.

Hand me a cigarette
I think I'm losing it,
I don't really know who I am anymore.
One day might be kind to me,
but the others are blind they see
small bits and pieces, the rest they ignore.

(Chorus)
C'mon cherry, we'll ride off to glory
though we might not remember too much of the story.
We'll hide from the shadows of the valleys we ride through,
and we'll carry that monkey
just as far as we have to.
Yeah!

If you can't understand
this angry old man
who is drowning in ego, but still swimming in bliss,
it's the minor afflictions
and the God Damned addictions
that haunt me and bruise me and make me like this.

I'll tell you my secret
if you promise to keep it;
the man you see standing here just isn't real.
In all the confusion
he became an illusion,
but hell, it don't matter it's just how I feel

(Chorus and big finish)
C'mon cherry, we'll ride off to glory
though we might not remember too much of the story.
We'll hide from the shadows of the valleys we ride through,
and we'll carry that monkey
just as far as we have to.
YEAH!

shattuck avenue

Oh those were the days
those awful days
filled with snakes
of desire and immoral
breakfasts
served in the dawn
off of Shattuck Avenue

That house of music
shaking and breathing
our dusty souls to life
wanton and nude
walking
calmly against traffic
off of Shattuck Avenue

Cowering wordless dogs
thrashing in the bushes
we were the animals
you spied on then
in wonder
gritting your teeth
off of Shattuck Avenue

Complacent bastards sleeping
with basement dwellers
food chain replacements
grinning and biting and drooling
palsied
by the wonder of lust
off of Shattuck Avenue

Tattooed sheep-less sheppards
gnawing dream leftovers
swill with garnish
pass the catsup
its dinner
served up pancake hot
off of Shattuck Avenue

Oh the gristle swallowed
direct from tendons
and muscle gone weak and bad
we still had to run
on legs
not meant for marathons
off of Shattuck Avenue

As careless stalkers preened
we'd dance looney
wet from sacrifice and sex
and sex and sex and sex
spent
dry as a bone dripping
off of Shattuck Avenue

Leave the restless wounded
lunch for the pursuers
the blood and brains
spackle and paint
bitter choices
for detectives snooping
off of Shattuck Avenue

Come hither young hearts
you mapless assholes
I'll draw you a picture
of my times there
my death
ranting and raving
off of Shattuck Avenue

pig

When I was a pig
musicians would beg
for piggy to heal all their wounds,
when I was a pig I bled in saloons,
I got hurt when I was a pig.

When I was a pig
girlies would crawl
to hotel rooms darkened and sweet,
when I was a pig I had all I could eat,
I wasn't shy when I was a pig.

When I was a pig
I spent every dime
in pursuit of wondrous things.
When I was a pig, I should have had wings.
I couldn't reach them when I was a pig.

When I was a pig
I tasted it all
from bourbons to powders through straws,
when I was a pig there weren't any laws,
I was evil when I was a pig.

When I was a pig
I did what I wanted
in every direction and back,
when I was a pig I might have lost track,
I didn't care when I was a pig.

When I was a pig
my heart felt like stone,
but it crumbled watching her dance,
when I was a pig I took one last chance
I thought she'd like me being a pig.

When I was a pig
she fucked up my life
by making me less than I was,
when I was a pig, that hurt and still does,
it's hard sometimes being a pig.

When I was a pig
she meant nothing to me,
it didn't hurt because I wouldn't feel,
when I was a pig nothing was real,
I wasn't ashamed of being a pig.

When I was a pig
I moved away
so nothing could hurt me again,
when I was a pig, not now but back then
I meant goodbye, but not as a pig.

church of roll god of rock

To all of my guitarists
and players of such
wrapping
simple
and tender notes
through those present
before our chapel
allow me to wash your hands
this
the holy water
of our time
fender twin
the voice of god
snaking through cable
slamming fist like
into the heads
and hearts
of those parishioners
still present
dancing at out altars
begging for sacrament
Holy father decibel
give us strength
through attendance
and through senhieser
lift up our voice
to the spires
of this church.

I will carry you my brothers and sisters
my priests
and together
we will
come rocking
to the fucking holy land.

roadie blues

one by one by one by one
those rock and rollers fall,
succumb
to the time that passes,
like a star falling
to the ground
unnoticed
by anyone.
You can pump that muscle
and the music rolls
where you want it to.
Don't stop pushing
or it'll roll back on you
and you're through,
then what would you do?
You might wake up one morning
and the music has left without you,
don't stop chasing that bus,
catch it or you're through,
then what would you do?
(A roadie whistles 'not fade away'
all the while his shoes are singing
'you can't always get what you want.')

condition human

there
we are,
weeping.

look
at us,
pathetic

solo
and sad,
precision

balanced
on life's
razor

quaking
and begging
relief

with
only whispers
near

chorus
of blood
within

we
remain that,
scared

ready
to fold,
buckle

from
the weight
outside.

look
at us
fakes,

there
we are,
weeping.

<u>crashing</u>

If your world
comes crashing down
so hard
that you can't hear a sound,
blame it on me,
it's my fault,
I'm around
if your world comes crashing down.

If your tears
they fall like rain
and your heart
just can't keep in the pain
I was wrong,
you were right,
I'm to blame
if your tears they fall like rain.

If you're mad
and you want me to leave,
I give up babe,
whatever you need.
If you're sad
and you want me to go,
I gave it my best
I thought you should know.

If my love
has done you wrong,
and your bad days
are just too god damned long,
turn your head,
look away,
I'll be gone
if my love has done you wrong.

devastation and sorrow

Devastation
waits
hard
for another lover's
hands
to soothe
the rent soul,
lips to rekindle
smoldering ruins
to love's flame
again.
Patient,
devastation is
always
waiting.

Sorrow
becomes
common
lurking behind shielded
hearts
beating slow
recovering from pain
and hurt
again and again
infinity.
Constant,
sorrow is
always
there.

<u>building the wall</u>

Brick by brick
I'll build this wall
closing myself off
from the world
so completely
I'll soon forget the likes of it.

Stone by stone
mortar and mud
we'll watch it grow
until height insures
I am totally
cut off from those emotional weaklings

that scrape and break
trying to manage
while begging to grasp
even one hint
of love and such
I've had enough of that for a while.

This entire row of rock
is for them
see how neatly
I fill the cracks
so lust and desire
hurt their heads banging against it.

These stones here
are for the women
and the unkept promises,
the lies and deceit
are the plumb
as straight as arrows these ramparts.

Here, we'll add a brick
or two for the bosses
and all the times
they lied about wage
or hours
that's all they're worth, just two.

I've seen some terrible walls
constructed haphazardly
without plans or thought
that come tumbling
at mere whispers
of regret, loneliness or sorrow

but mine, every inch
constructed with vision
and future plans
of what will be
here, alone
behind this wall of mine.

The purpose is
to keep them out
even though some
might try still
they'll be Up Against it!
what a thrill it'll be watching them cower

So brick by brick
stone by stone
I build this mighty wall
to keep you bastards
out of my life
I wont even answer the phone any more.

where

I once lived
where summertime boiled away confusion and doubt
leaving smudges
of complacency
across a land dried like tobacco,
where folks raised tents
like flags
to show themselves off to the world;
state fairs meant to replace farmer's dirt
with big city cobwebs,
where a million billion beer swilling
slow walking rednecks
wallowed in the corn dogged cotton candied dust
where corn dogs were king,
where $7.00 might win
a dimes worth of painted plastic toy
for young hearts
walking the midway
dressed in gossip,
where children were dizzied
by screaming machines
shooting faster
running further
and climbing higher
than every rocket ever made,
where mothers and fathers
remembered stolen kisses
that ultimately led

to the wide eyed screams of tilt o' whirled children
doomed to the same memories,
where blue ribbons took futures
from back road dreariness
to main street glory
and sad eyed animals might,
for an instant,
see freedom through victory,
where it all ended up hamburger
chops
and corndogs anyway.

iowa night

Listen to the rumbling steel,
the creaking of the wood
speaking things of far away
in whispers, dead of night
I should
follow the rails into the black,
the whistle as it moans,
but fear of dark
and death from cold
will keep me safe at home.

anytown usa

difficult to believe
that it could get that quiet
when someone new
entered the truck stop café,
all of the brazen eyes
following until
a seat is found,
coffee is poured,
menu offered.

then
the chitchat continues,
each conversation
penetratingly clear.

doreen is in the hospital
again
poor girl
and her mother has the kids

the damn dog got out
and terrorized
the entire neighborhood
again

the sister
of the waitress
is preggers again
and he doesn't know

he isn't going to spend
all of that damn money
for a new tractor
no way

and doreen might
just loose
the next one
if she isn't careful

he can fix the engine
but he has to drive
all the way out there
to get the friggin parts

and they'll
shoot the damn thing
if it bites
anyone else

quieres fumar?
the busboy
waved off
by the cook

and she started
popping them out
when she was 16
she's such a slut

quiero comer
and the cook
starts eggs
for the busboy

we'd have to take
a third
on the house
just to buy the damn thing

you want
more coffee
or
are you ok?

my conversation
is short
and to the point
check please

and it is again
eerily silent
as I grab my smokes from the counter
and walk outside,
back into anytown usa,
the rental,
the airport
to home.

iowa poem

Midnight lightning flashes
jeering,
taunting the parched fields below.
Crickets dine
to cricket song,
last meals in the dying grass.

i'm starving mom

I gotta eat something mom.
I gotta eat something.
hungry
hungry
no place to eat
what should I do
you always knew
the answers
I have no money
and I'm on the streets
and I gotta eat something mom
I gotta eat something
I look in the windows mom
all those restaurants
mom they're eating well
and I remember all those times
when I was late for dinner
but you warmed up my food
I gotta eat something mom
I gotta eat something.
I'm tired and I have no place to sleep
and I'm thinking of you in the kitchen
and my stomach hurts
and the soup kitchen is closed
and the police chased me away from
the garbage cans
I gotta eat something mom
I gotta eat something.

I remember when the icebox was full
and I had my pick
and I'd stand there while you shouted
to close the damn door
or the food would spoil
I miss that now mom
I just couldn't make up my mind
staring at all those offerings
that I only dream about now
I gotta eat something mom
I gotta eat something.

I'm laying down in this alley now mom
maybe I can get to the soup kitchen tomorrow
maybe I'll find 20 cents and by a stamp
and write you saying that I'm living in style
or maybe I'll spend it on something to eat
with a promise to write some other day
because I gotta eat something mom
I gotta eat something.
I'm tired
and I gotta eat something.

living in dallas 1979

Rent: $75.00 per month
Utilities: $18.00 per month
Income: $63.00 per month
I always had money left over
after moving into
the roach and rat infested duplex next door to Richard, Penny and
Clark.
Maybe it was the
speed
that screwed up my bookkeeping
or maybe
it was the 3 gorgeous
20 year olds living next door
who realized my plight
and left the shades up
or basked nude in the back of their roach and rat infested duplex
next door
less than 15 feet away.
I learned to say grace
in 105 ° weather
over a $0.98 frozen dinner
cooked on hot plate
because the stove had one day
become a roach crematorium.
I drank from the hose outside
because the sink was a recreation area for the roaches and rats
a swimming pool for the vermin roommates,
and unless Richard, Penny and Clark

scored
and there was beer and more speed
my time was spent
lying sweating in a bed facing the 20 year olds
masturbating with them,
feeling my weight drop like a stone,
listening to my stomach groan
the only sound in that roach and rat infested duplex in the middle
of the night
unless you counted the smothered moans
coming from bedrooms of the roach and rat infested duplex next
door
as the 3 gorgeous 20 year olds
shades up
masturbated with me.
give us a kiss
before the roaches and rats
carry off this empty
carcass.
give us a kiss love.

4 different street people

Visions of tragedy
I have visions
there's nothing I can do about it
it happens to me
everyday
so I stand
out on this corner
almost all the time
hoping I'll get lost in the crowd
and satan won't find me
he could make me hurt someone
or maybe even hurt
myself
again.

Visions of paradise
I have visions
There's nothing I want to do about it
it happens to me
everyday
so I stand
out on this corner
with the word of god
written on my placard screaming at the crowd
knowing satan can't touch me
as long as I praise the lord
I praise god
myself
for you

Visions of beauty
I have visions
There's nothing else I can think about
it happens to me
every second
so I sit
in these rooms
with my dollar bills
wishing that was me on the screen
trying not to touch myself
as long as I got money
I watch
the show
all day

Visions of people
I see visions
There's nothing here for me to eat
so I know
that they're not
really there
I ask the ghosts walking by
for some money
I know that if I ate
something
I'd feel myself
becoming whole
something else
me

memories of the burrito bitch

Sometimes
I forget to eat breakfast
and lunch
and the day passes and
the time finds me
sitting at my nasty
cluttered desk
with the cat
chewing on my feet
smoking cigarette
after cigarette
until
I get this sensation
that unleashes a flood
of memories
of Dallas
in the late seventies
when I was so
awfully
god damned hungry
and didn't have a dime
and my days were spent
walking
through this small park
on a trail that ended
at a busy street
right in front of
a taco joint.

I would sit
on the bus stop bench
and stare at that place
for hours
occasionally begging
and braving
the assault from the
200-pound woman
that spent her days
making tortillas
and chasing me away
and screaming at me in Spanish.
That winter,
still penniless
and about to be evicted
at Christmas time
I remember having visions,
starvation does that sometimes
and I was walking
and dreaming
and I didn't even feel
the cruelest winter gale
the city had felt in years.
I ended up like I always did
at the end of that trail
in front of that taco joint.
But this time
on the bus stop bench
there was a bag
hot to the touch
smelling like sweet greasy mexico
filled with an easy 2 pounds
of the finest fare
that place had to offer.
A napkin note simply said

"Feliz Navidad"
and as the bus pulled away across the street
the cook,
that beautiful, old burrito-making bitch
was blowing me a kiss
from the back window.
What a fucking picnic.
I remember those things now
as I go to make my first meal
of the day.

kissing the seasons

dead calendars,
the shear force of numbers
multiplied by
winters of desperation
and summers of lust
somehow joined at the hip,
a matter of time
between flesh
and wetness,
where does it go
pray tell

all of this
could be insignificant
and wandering,
loosely based
upon fictions
none of us have dared to read,
or write
yet
and still
the autobiography
is essential here,
and every place else
we dare to dream

I knew him once,
the king of man
or simple sorcerer
tangoing
with the absurd,
there are still occasional reflections,
and superb recipes
flittering
on tongue tips,
caged dances
surrounded by music
that instills madness
and raises
desires long dead

Spring weddings
torn between autumn
and death,
it's all legal tender and binding,
allocated and allowed
by the laws
of past mistakes
that whisper to us all
while we bathe
in splendors not really meant
for mortals,
or us
less than that,
shall we dance my friend

we'll spike this day
with euphoria
and glance to muted horizons
with prayers and such,
give me the flags
and banners,
together we can walk that mile
above water
blown along
by the winds of faith
or forethought,
hand in hand

but now
the vagueness of such things,
the illusions of the heart,
temperate at best
still suffering under temptation
are lost,
faint but final
the glow dies during a weary evening
chambers cleared
and sterile,
the whole of the thing
dissipates
and evaporates
until all there is
is kissing the seasons

amor de buenos aires

"Quiero irme."
"Donde?"
"Alla"
"Porque?"
"Seguir mi corazon."
My simple Spanish
made her smile.
"Un beso de Argentina,"
and her lips butterfly across my mouth,
tongue searching for nectar.
My hands reach to cup
breasts silhouetted by the lights
of Calle Arenales
half neon,
half setting sun.
Her scent mingles
with neighborhood pastry shops
stealing through the open window
our hands, fingers, mouths
exploring the combination of delicacies.
"Te quiero, te deseo."
Her face above me,
we join,
communicating in rhythmic,
speechless motion;
drops of sweat
washing away any words
that might have been written between us.
There is no language lost.

skopje dreams

Sanja dancing
on the dirty sidewalk
while bent backs
with wrinkled eyes
stare wide
with a sparkle
not quite sure if the yoke
they wore
would allow them
to join in.
"It is an old
country"
she says
doubting her own words
could describe,
watching
while a 70 year old woman,
bent back,
wrinkled eyes,
hands me
a beautiful rose
gleefully jabbering
in Cyrillic syllables
the entire time.
Sanja translates
and says
"The flower
is for our wedding bed."

All of those curious
bent backs
with wrinkled eyes
sparkling
proud to say 4 words
in english
while being as hospitable
as an old communist can,
where are you from
and
why are you here
the most frequent forms
of conversation
for the few tourists
wandering the streets
in search of
Alexander
and King Philip
and the Turks
and the castles
that seem to disappear
as you get close.
Like Sanja.

We kiss over whiskey,
in bars
with straight backs,
with younger eyes,
staring.
We make love
in the hotel
far from the real Macedonia
with the pains
and growls

and dirt
and history
that showers me
with Tito memories
while I watch her dress
and leave for home.

holland song, or an idiot goes to a'dam

Please come to Holland
I'll make you a sinner
you can buy me some drinks
take me out for a dinner
and we'll spend some time
in a red light hotel room,

so I'm going to Holland
because she wrote me a letter
and I might not return
if I get used to the weather
so don't hold your breath
or expect me home too soon.

I'm leaving her
she's leaving me
we're leaving each other behind,
my god it's tough
but we've both had enough
of not having our own piece of mind.

(Goedenavond, hoe gaat het? Mijn naam is . . ., hoe heet u? Mag
ik heir gaan zitten?
Wilt u wat drinken? Jij bent mooi, Ik hou van jou, heb jij zin om
te neuken?)

Don't go to Holland
if you want a lover,
it'll all break your heart
one way or the other
and you could wind up drunk and
howling at the moon.

But I went back to Holland
thinking that I could win her
if I bought her some drinks
and took her out for a dinner
but she left me alone
in this red light hotel room.

I'm leaving her,
she's leaving me,
we're leaving each other you see,
it's much too tough
to call the bluff
but not quite as tough being free.

another holland song

Old man walking the canal at dawn,
there's a pretty woman with a red dress on
hookers, hustlers, part time dealers,
it's getting hard to take
it's getting hard to take.

And I'm screaming from my hotel room
into the streets below
"Who'll quench my thirst for lust and love
and miss me when I go?"
And the idle hours
and longer days
start blending into one
till sacrifice and broken hearts
mean nothing cause you're done.

Where do you go when the sun shines bright
to hide yourself until it's night,
some other lovers' darkened bedroom?
it's getting hard to wait
it's getting hard to wait.

And I'm falling from my hotel room
into the streets below,
I hate to spoil your perfect day
but I really have to go.
The idle hours and longer days
are turning into one

and sacrifice and fucking tears
mean nothing cause I'm done,
and I'm falling,
and falling
and falling.

to dance in morocco

Sands of Islam
so piercing,
quiet.
A million years of sun
in whispers
over golden dunes
stretched in watery waves
as far as the eye can see.
Running through my fingers
every grain crashes
splashing ageless dust
rejoining oceans of Moroccan desert
lapping my sandaled feet.
I danced on that mountain of sand
crazy from fear and heat
thinking the blistering stillness
would devour me
praying the days veiled faces
would forgive.
Swaying
to Berber hypnotists,
mesmerized,
I only now remember
that I was consumed.

morocco night

if silence
was actually golden
precious metal
tangible
pieces of ore
glittering,
this empty
quiet
moroccan night
would bury me
under
a mass
of wealth

all of you

Of course
I remember you
you were the one
that screamed
in orgasm
eyes rolling
bucking
definitely
not thinking of
shopping
or nails
being done
and you,
you are
the one that cried
when I told you
goodbye
and you
are the strange one
that wanted
your sister to watch
and you
yeah, you,
you just wanted to watch
then there's you,
I said you
were the best
but you weren't

and you,
over there,
did you ever
get your wish
about the dog?
what about you
that barely moved
and you
that time on the bus
and of course
you
and your three girlfriends
for three days
we played
and then
you and you
and you
meant nothing
but you
you were
special
you meant something
you hurt me
when you left
you were
so beautiful
and you
you bitch,
I had to get a shot
and you
were there
when I really needed someone
you,
you were the best
for a while

until
you came along
and changed it all
and you wanted it
all the time
and then there was you
so loving, giving
and you
what a kinky thing
all that food
in bed
and you wanted
my friend
and you thanked me
and you were the one
who let me tie you up
of course you
didn't want your husband
to know
and you
made me do it
so the neighbors
could watch and you
wanted it everywhere
and you left me
for her
and you were
totally crazy and
I had to call the police

but you
were the difficult one
do you still have the pictures?
you were the one
I saw in the porn movie
after you disappeared
and you,
and you
were the one
that fucked me up
so bad
I'm still
not
quite
right
you,
of course
I remember you
what was
your name
again?

it's over

Just damaged goods
why do you think
they all look at you,
they talk about you
behind a mask
behind the walls
behind your back,
you had something once
but now
you're just damaged goods,
if she aint good enough
then why would
someone else want you
it's a joke
maybe you started it
maybe she started it
but now it's a joke
that everyone knows
and they repeat it
to your face
forgetting that
you're the one
it's about
and it's just
a depressing outing
where they look at you
when they first walk
into the darkened

arena
perfumed and searching
and its ok until someone
tells the fucking joke
then
you're just some
wasted bastard
they can ignore
you're out of the game
motherfucker
why are you even here
oh right,
buy us a drink
then leave us alone
you wasted, useless
bastard
oh
wait,
have you heard the one about . . .?

look at life

Snowflakes fall
down on the frozen river,
my breath is fog
on the ice cold air,
the sky is cloudy
and it's likely to be stormy,
but all I know
is that you're not there.

Little children
dressing up so warmly,
they run out to play
in the new fallen snow,
but I'll stay inside
next to this fireplace, drinking whiskey,
getting drunk because I just don't know

how to
look at life
as it twists and turns around me.
I fell in love
and then got hurt real bad.
I stumbled and fell
now I can't function like I used to,
can't start all over
can't forget what I had.

I can picture you now
you're laying out in sunny weather,
rubbing that oil
where the sun don't shine.
You know, I still recall
that we used to live together
and now you're giving away
what used to be mine

and you say,
look at life
as it twists and turns around you,
you say you fell in love
and then got hurt real bad,
I saw you stumble and fall
now you wont function like you used to,
you better start all over
and forget what you had.
Look at life . . .

after her

the fear
of the unknown
should always be
less
than the fear of regret
and so we loved
and that consumed us,
both
burnt in that fiery passion,
all the while
we were eaten whole,
chewed,
swallowed by the denial
of everything
we were not together.
We became
mathematics,
the sum of two parts
ignorantly added
by closing our eyes
and scribbling numbers
on a page
and
for a moment,
a while,
for a time
we were
invisible and invincible

armored,
and
we lowered our weapons
and discovered
buried treasures.
We danced.
We learned.

Time passed
just like water
and we washed our hands
of the mistakes we made
ignored the slights,
hid the anger,
and fear
and desires
in small unkept closets
that required walls
that we
built
and fortified
until
we both faced brick and mortar
instead of ourselves
again
and we bruised,
broke and splintered
trying to climb
that fortress

so
we parted.
we left.
we stopped.
Every sound,
sight
and feeling wrapped,
packaged
and put away
and I sat,
and I sat in that nothingness
for
a moment,
a while,
for a time.

love goes away

So much time passes
unnoticed, uncared for
unrealized
reality slipping a bit,
words run back
away from the tip
of the tongue
the teeth clenching
jaw tightened
and eyes closed.
Being finished with love
at this early age
(ah, but then it finds you)
no longer searching
I can feel it leave my body
after a period of time.
time and the desire
to track it
watch it
desire shoots through
clean through
like a gunshot
cauterizing
leaving nothing but a hole
emptiness
I am Buddha in this sense
meditating on
the nothingness and

emptiness
and all of the emotion
the wasted time
becomes more of a memory
that falls out of the hole
created by letting all of it go
and after days
months
all the time unnoticed
uncared for and unrealized
becomes a reality
and the words climb back
into my mouth
and prepare to spring
from the tip of my tongue,
the jaw and teeth
unclench and the eyes open
waiting for the next gunshot.
ready to duck
this time.

the rest

I
can only
try to guess
how you feel
now
after you
said
you
weren't
like the rest
and
found out
that
you are;
does it
hurt?

Good.

the therapist

I went to a therapist
for a bit.
I was angry and drinking
I was sad and drinking
I thought maybe
I was depressed.
The therapist started by asking
"Why did you come here?"
I told her
because a woman hurt me
and I hurt her back,
nothing physical.

She asked me
"Why do you think you drink?"
I told her
because I can't stop
falling in love with women
and then I told her
about all of my
relationships,
all of the horrible
beautiful
painful
loving
tortured relationships I'd been in
and she kept nodding
and writing things down
without looking at me.

Then she asked me
"Why do you think
all of your lovers have been so young?"
I told her it was because
I was getting older
then she showed me a picture
of the presidents wife
on the cover of a magazine
and asked
"Do you think she's beautiful?"
and I said yes
but I thought the presidents
daughter was more beautiful
then she asked me
quite seriously
"Would you fuck the presidents wife
because she is beautiful?"
and I said yes
but I'd prefer to fuck the daughter.

The therapist said
I was afraid of getting old
and it was common,
kind of a mid-life crisis
and then she asked
if I had ever been attracted to an older woman
say,
her age.
She didn't look that old
and was very attractive so I said
I'd fuck you
and that was pretty much the end
of that therapy session.

<u>Pussy</u>

Is that all you ever think about?
Pussy?
Doesn't that make you
crazy?
No, I answer.
Pussy
is what made me
crazy
to begin with.
Just like
going home.
It's a
short
walk.
Hey
look
at
the
redhead.

touch

Do you
feel
my heart
beating against your skin
as you lie,
back to me,
nestled,
a spoon,
the rising
and falling
of your
breathing
brings you
closer
than
I have been
to anyone
in some time,
and
my hand
not so graceful
on your hip,
thigh
wants you closer still
so you can feel
that dizzy blood
swimming.
Dream

and dream
love
and when you
awake,
press close.
I
will be waiting.

love songs for the non-existent woman

I see your face on billboards
and magazines
captured,
frozen,
as the city passes by
trying to inhale your perfumed stillness.

A million heartbeats walk by
dancing in crazy steps
splashing shadows
and breath
across your pictures,
lips parted,
eyes closed,
you breathe back,
warming me in the crowd

Scattered papers tackle unsuspecting passersby
ignorant
but glowing fresh
from the slap of noon.
You whisper and beckon
throwing sunny diamond glares.
I oblige.

Reaching,
I lift my feet and fly,
grasping at the bliss,
the temptation,
the secrets
that are the beauty of you
but come away empty handed
again.

love songs for the non-existent woman 2

Another day begins
the world is turning
so it seems.
As sharpened shadows creep
reality
competes with dreams.
From the edge of sleep I see
you soft and silent
lying near.
I reach my hand to you
and call your name
so you will hear.
You gently turn and smile
your morning scent
is pure desire.
I touch your lips with mine
rekindling
prior evenings' fire.
As arms and legs entwine
salty sweetness
begs to flow.
But then you disappear
from sudden bursts
of mornings' glow.
It's then that I awake
alone and cold
still quite aware.
You were my dream again

and
never really there.
And I remember why
I hesitate
before I sleep,
the fear of lying there
with loving visions
I can't keep.
Another day begins,
the world is turning
so it seems.

the new thing

while others kiss
behind
blackened windows
love songs whispering
we debate,
touching lips
chaste
almost,
trading information
governed lust
barely allowing
a touch,
we are new
and
sleeping alone
in stiff beds
and
we
play
and plan,
what
if.

jessica lee

Are you there?
are you reading this?
your father
wants to know
though
you might think
I wasn't dad
much,
and I know
I wasn't there
for you
but then again
where were you?
I guess
mom
didn't think
I'd care
but don't think
for even a second
I didn't,
I wondered
from the moment
she told me
you were there
inside of her
what would happen
between us.

I never had a chance
really
as if our lives
were pre-determined,
at least it seemed so
after we parted
and I chose a road
your mother
would never drive,
even though the stops
along the way
might have been similar
the maps we used
while you grew
were from different countries
entirely,
all those different paths
we might have
traveled together
lost now.
As the years die
between us
mute and cold
because of circumstance
or slight of hand
you should know
that this void
has been bequeathed
by both of us
your parents
she
unwilling
unwitting
or wily
and I,

frightened
and too ashamed
to try
and claim
your love.

sagadin

when we look
in the mirror
some of the ghosts
we can scare off,
some
are just that,
invisible,
then,
there is
sagadin
this woman
who changed me
so completely
when I was so
impressionable
and
young
and there she was
so perfect
and she didn't even know it
and she tasted like
a wine
I will never
know again,
and
she didn't even know
she was drinkable
and she slew me

and
she threw my
sorry
carcass
on a fire
that still burns today
and
I think about
this woman
with sorrow
and love
and lust
that can never
ever
be repeated
in my life
and when we talk
I wonder
if she knows
after all this time
that she,
sagadin,
is the only reason
that I still
have the balls
to exist,
that worthy quest
as a man,
knowing that
everything
since
and until,
is
a whisper
of what I felt

then.
Just a whisper,
she was,
is,
all that,
and even more,
love.

cleo

In a crowd
somewhere
I can't tell
because the surroundings
have blurred
and slipped away
other voices
slight echoes,
then nothing,
my focus
on the movement
of your lips
the tongue
past the teeth
the sharp nose
as it meets
those penetrating,
serious
eyes
that I pray
will meet mine
so I can confess,
and the way
your hand
glides gracefully
taking forever
to reach and play
with your hair,

and I say your name
just as I am shaken awake,
time to go
and the moment
is gone.
Just like you.
Cleo.

<u>be</u>

Everyone should fantasize
from time
to time.
Those glasses,
the pink ones,
one size fits all
simple prescription
or
you can close your eyes
and
get really serious
about it.
Lay back
in the grass
unfettered
and glow,
size
and scope
and subscription
irrelevant
my friend,
be.

reality

facing the day's
many temptations
blind
as a bat
somehow
unable
or
unwilling
to focus
just so,
dream hangovers,
additions
to the clutter
making decisions
and judgment
nearly
impossible,
facing a day
like this
being cloudy
as an iowa november
or as foggy
as any san francisco morning
makes slow going
and
false starts
frequent,
even hellos

to acquaintances
jumble
and though I'm sure
she is there,
sitting near,
what
could I possibly
say
or do
now?

desire

we all wallow in it
submerged
ankle,
waist,
neck deep
and
we don't even know it,
wading through
the desire,
mired,
thicker
than mud
or blood,
the very cause of it
all,
everything
we are
and will ever be
is our
own desire
and so
we fail
and lose
all we could be,
us

the path

We all walk
on unsteady feet,
unsure
of the ground
on which we tread,
attempting
to balance
on narrow passage,
careful
not to muddy
the shoes
that protect
our delicate soles
all the while
unaware,
that how we stride
realizes
our destination
but usually
forgets
the path,
step
lightly.

hope

Even at my worst,
coked and bruised
drunk and stoned
walking frozen
and empty
I could always see
a dim
glimmer,
peripheral,
ready to shine anew
with the brilliance
of a million suns
into my
miserable
fucking
life.

After having hoped
so many times
and having
none of it,
I realize now
that the light is still there
and
I can hold it
warm
in my hands
any time

I want
with no religious overtone
or tilt
what so ever
and with that hope
comes love
and
compassion
and patience,
and so much more.

As the battle
dies,
life,
and I on occasion
take count,
breathe,
I remember
the worst times
right along
with the best
and now
I will live
knowing
there is
and always will be
a glimmer
just
over there.

Say goodnight Kevyn

Photo shoot concept by Kevyn Clark
Photographer: Brett Barclay/Barclayarts
Assistant Photographer: Bill Long/Barclayarts
Models: "The Babe" Lisa Martinez
"The Guy In The Suit" Kevyn Clark
Rubber duck and knife by Barclayarts

Cartoon concept by Kevyn Clark
Cartoon artwork: Robert Therrien Jr.

Thanks to The Black Watch Bar, Los Gatos California for the alley
and the booze

Heartfelt thanks to Robert Hunter
for his words

Printed in the United States
3054